Especially for

_____

From

_____

Date

_____

25
Christmas
Blessings

Scripture quotations marked KJV are taken from the King James Version of the Bible.

Scripture quotations marked NIV are taken from the HOLY BIBLE, NEW INTERNATIONAL VERSION®. NIV®. Copyright © 1973, 1978, 1984, 2011 by Biblica, Inc.™ Used by permission. All rights reserved worldwide.

Scripture quotations marked NLT are taken from the *Holy Bible*. New Living Translation copyright© 1996, 2004, 2007 by Tyndale House Foundation. Used by permission of Tyndale House Publishers, Inc. Carol Stream, Illinois 60188. All rights reserved.

Scripture quotations marked NASB are taken from the New American Standard Bible, © 1960, 1962, 1963, 1968, 1971, 1972, 1973, 1975, 1977, 1995 by The Lockman Foundation. Used by permission.

Scripture quotations marked MSG are from *THE MESSAGE*. Copyright © by Eugene H. Peterson 1993, 1994, 1995, 1996, 2000, 2001, 2002. Used by permission of NavPress Publishing Group.

Scripture quotations marked ESV are taken from The Holy Bible, English Standard Version®, copyright © 2001 by Crossway Bibles, a publishing ministry of Good News Publishers. Used by permission. All rights reserved.

Scripture quotations marked NCV are taken from the New Century Version of the Bible, copyright © 2005 by Thomas Nelson, Inc. Used by permission. All rights reserved.

Scripture quotations marked CEV are from the Contemporary English Version, Copyright © 1995 by American Bible Society. Used by permission.

Scripture quotations marked NKJV are taken from the New King James Version®. Copyright © 1982 by Thomas Nelson, Inc. Used by permission. All rights reserved.

Scripture quotations marked AMP are taken from the Amplified® Bible, © 1954, 1958, 1962, 1964, 1965, 1987 by The Lockman Foundation. Used by permission.

Published by Barbour Books, an imprint of Barbour Publishing, Inc., P.O. Box 719, Uhrichsville, Ohio 44683, www.barbourbooks.com

Our mission is to publish and distribute inspirational products offering exceptional value and biblical encouragement to the masses.

 Member of the
Evangelical Christian
Publishers Association

Printed in the United States of America.

25
Christmas
Blessings

An Inspiring Countdown to Christmas!

✳ ✳ ✳

Dena Dyer

BARBOUR BOOKS
An Imprint of Barbour Publishing, Inc.

Introduction

It's the most wonderful time of the year. . .

Christmastime brings out a variety of emotions. Some people feel antsy thinking about the expectations of the season, and the resulting "to do" list (buy, wrap, bake). Others get practically giddy at the thought of more time with family members, sparkling Christmas lights, and contemplative Advent traditions. Some of us dread the season because we've lost loved ones, and the hole they've left behind feels more cavernous this time of year.

Whatever your feelings about Christmas, I pray that this devotional encourages you—first and foremost—that God is truly with you. After all, the name *Emmanuel* means "God is with us." Jesus' incarnation ultimately led to the resurrection, so death doesn't have the final say.

Through readings, prayers, scriptures, and service ideas, the goal of *25 Christmas Blessings* is to re-center our gaze on Jesus. When we become Christ-centered, we become more aware of our blessings than of our problems. His Holy Spirit then leads us to reach out to others and *become* a blessing. As a result, God gives us more peace and joy than we ever imagined.

Speaking of joy, I want to thank my friends on social media and my students at Lakeside Baptist Academy for helping me complete the 250 service ideas. Their generous spirit helped me greatly!

I pray you have a merry Christmas, but more than that, I pray that you see Jesus more clearly, and feel His love more deeply, than ever before.

Be Thankful

Give thanks to the Lord, for he is good,
for his steadfast love endures forever.
PSALM 136:1 ESV

Be Thankful

*Therefore, as you received Christ Jesus the Lord,
so walk in him, rooted and built up in him and
established in the faith, just as you were taught,
abounding in thanksgiving.*
Colossians 2:6–7 esv

As Christmas approached, newly-widowed Darlene
felt discouraged. The past year had been particularly
difficult financially, and she didn't know how she
would pay for presents for her children. The kids told
her that presents for their teachers were expected at
their school, and she was part of a gift exchange at
work. After attempting to reconcile her checkbook
with the mounting bills, she became even more
frustrated. Hot tears coursed down her cheeks.

Suddenly, the Holy Spirit whispered to her
spirit: "Pray. Don't worry. Remember how I've taken
care of you."

Darlene wiped her face and bowed her head.
"Lord," she murmured, "You know my situation.
You know that I don't have a lot of extra money.

And at this time of year, the expenses pile up, and expectations are overwhelming. Please help me discern between what's necessary and unnecessary."

After praying and reading scripture for a few moments, Darlene felt prompted to turn on worship music and make a list of the multiple, miraculous ways God had provided for her over the last few years. Then she took out a piece of paper and brainstormed a few simple gifts she and the kids could make for teachers. A closeout sale earlier in the year, which she had taken advantage of, had filled a closet in her bedroom with simple, small items she could put together for a fellow employee.

When worry turns to worship, God works—and wisdom wins.

Father, thank You for Your provision. Help me not
to worry, but to instead be consistently aware of
all the ways You take care of me and my family.
I know You are faithful to provide all that I need.
Forgive me for doubting You and—too often—
taking matters into my own hands. Your ways are
better, Lord. Your love is steadfast. Help me to live
a life of love and abound in thanksgiving.

*"As surely as you harvest your grain and grapes,
you will eat your bread with thankful hearts,
and you will drink your wine in my temple."*
ISAIAH 62:9 CEV

10 Ways to Bless Others This Christmas:

1. Write a note (or draw a picture) and give it to each of your family members, listing the specific characteristics for which you are thankful.
2. Give a thank-you card to your church custodian.
3. Leave a small gift in the mailbox for your mail carrier.
4. Help children in your family write a short note to their teacher and place it in a stocking (filled with office supplies or a gift certificate) on the instructor's desk before school lets out for Christmas.
5. Give a basket of homemade goodies with a thank-you card to the workers at your local convenience store (they often have to work on special holidays).
6. Contact your local military support group and ask what kind of care packages they are planning for the holidays; enlist family and friends to help fill at least one or two packages.

7. Make a gift basket for a veteran you know to thank them for their service.
8. With friends, roommates, or family members, pick out a gift to give to Jesus this Christmas. Consider adopting a family in need and buying presents for them, as well as stocking their pantry.
9. Begin a gratitude journal (or jar, basket, etc.) as a family or study group. Every so often, read it together and praise the Lord for what He's done.
10. Start a "thankful" thread on your social media account. Post one thing each day during Advent that you're grateful for and ask people to join in.

·············· 2 ··············

Believe

*"Blessed is she who has believed that
the Lord would fulfill his promises to her!"*
LUKE 1:45 NIV

Believe

And Jesus said to him, "'If You can?'
All things are possible to him who believes."
MARK 9:23 NASB

When we look around our sin-sick world, it's difficult
to remember that God sent Jesus into the world not
only to redeem the world but also to restore it. One
day all broken things will be made new. All nations
will be at peace; all women, men, and children will
bow to the King of kings, and He will reign justly.

For now, we're like the Israelites in the 400 silent
years between the last word of God's prophets and
the announcement of the birth of Jesus: confused,
full of doubt and despair. We feel forgotten. *Is God*
really coming back? we wonder. *Are His promises really*
true?

They are. One day, the Bible says, Jesus will
destroy hunger, devastation, and degradation. He will
deal justice to those who have captured and pillaged
and tortured; He will give peace to the victims of
cruel oppression.

Satan roams the earth for now, but soon, our righteous King will destroy him and all his demons. Humans are victims—for now—of his schemes, but not for long. God will cup our faces in His hands, brush the tears off our cheeks, and kiss our heads as He holds us close.

Our King is coming, just as He came over 2,000 years ago to a virgin who found favor. He is coming in truth and power. Until then, we hold onto God's hands as He holds our hearts. And we share our faith, so that others will find the hope they have longed for.

Abba Father, I long for Your return. It's hard to hold onto faith when I see my brothers and sisters suffering. It's hard to believe in Your Kingdom when others betray me, and You, and seem to get away with it. Give me faith in the midst of my doubt, Lord. Give me the strength to believe when others turn away, and let Your Spirit renew my hope when the days are long. Give me boldness to share Your peace and joy with others.

He will swallow up death [in victory; He will abolish death forever]. And the Lord God will wipe away tears from all faces; and the reproach of His people He will take away from off all the earth; for the Lord has spoken it.
ISAIAH 25:8 AMP

10 Ways to Bless Others This Christmas:

1. Listen to and pray with someone who's having trouble holding onto their faith.
2. Give a book/box filled with Bible promises to a family member or friend.
3. Bring your family members or friends along with you to sing and play musical instruments (or read/tell stories) at a local children's hospital.
4. Post a different Bible verse on your social media account every day of Advent.
5. Tell your children the story of the real Saint Nicholas, a follower of Christ.
6. Host a subdued "Blue Christmas" service at your church for those who are grieving.
7. Skype with a long-distance friend or family member on Christmas Day.
8. Write encouraging notes to your kids and spouse and hang them on a special "God and I Believe in You" tree throughout the holiday season.
9. Ask someone you work with about their Christmas traditions or about Santa Claus. Pray about the opportunity to transition into

a conversation about Jesus, if it's appropriate.

10. Take communion with roommates, friends, or family on Christmas Eve. Talk about the reason God gave Jesus to the world that first Christmas.

·········· 3 ··········

Pray

But me, I'm not giving up. I'm sticking around to see what GOD will do. I'm waiting for God to make things right. I'm counting on God to listen to me.
MICAH 7:7 MSG

Pray

*Answer their prayers from
heaven and give them victory.*
1 KINGS 8:45 CEV

The weeks leading up to Christmas are often hectic.
School programs, church activities, and preparation
for holiday gatherings take a lot of energy and time.
But let's not neglect moments of quiet prayer during
Christmas though. Prayer is too important of a
spiritual discipline to let it slide.

Have you ever heard someone say, "All we can
do is pray"? Why do we think that prayer is the
least important of all the acts of service we can give
to someone in crisis? A meal can feed a friend's
physical hunger, but prayer—and the peace that we
impart when we lift someone up to the Father—
feeds a spiritual need.

Also, we can pray any time of the day or night in
any place we find ourselves. Prayer is a powerful tool
against discouragement and, besides the Word of
God, it is the main weapon we have to fight off the

enemy of our souls. Intercessory prayer is a way to minister to those who might never hear our witness or accept our testimony. James 5:16 (KJV) says, "The effectual fervent prayer of a righteous man availeth much."

Ask God for the desire and discipline to pray for your immediate, extended, and church families. Use scriptures—especially those in Paul's letters—to personalize prayers for friends who need encouragement, faith, and endurance. Pray for missionaries and pastors in your circles, and don't forget to intercede for local, state, and national government officials.

Creator God, You made me to know You and find deep fulfillment in You. I praise You for the gift of prayer, in which I can fellowship with You and receive daily strength for my needs. Give me the desire and discipline through Your Holy Spirit to seek You diligently in prayer. When I feel overwhelmed by my schedule, let me turn to You as a respite from the rush, instead of rushing through prayer to get to something else. I love You, Lord. Thank You for loving me.

My voice shalt thou hear in the morning, O Lord;
in the morning will I direct my prayer
unto thee, and will look up.
PSALM 5:3 KJV

10 Ways to Bless Others This Chri

1. Prayer walk through your neighbo... around your child's school and sports fields.
2. Put all the Christmas cards you receive in a bowl or box. Pick one from the container each day and pray for the sender(s) of the card, and. . .
3. Send a note to the person(s) you prayed for, telling them that you remembered them during your prayer time.
4. When you go out to eat, before you pray for the meal, ask your server if you can pray for something specific for them.
5. Pray for a different family or church member each day during Advent.
6. Give manicures at a local senior center and ask the recipients if and how you can pray for them.
7. Ask the ministry staff at your church for specific prayer requests.
8. Post "How can I pray for you?" on your Facebook wall or Twitter feed.
9. Make a family/small group prayer journal, in which you record dated prayer requests—and answers.

10. Write a letter to a missionary telling them you are praying for them.

········ 4 ········

Give

*"Give away your life; you'll find life given back,
but not merely given back—given back with bonus
and blessing. Giving, not getting, is the way.
Generosity begets generosity."*
LUKE 6:38 MSG

Give

*You will be enriched in every way to be
generous in every way, which through
us will produce thanksgiving to God.*
2 CORINTHIANS 9:11 ESV

Felicity, her husband, Tom, and their twin sons, Finn
and Jake, decided to serve their elderly neighbor by
putting up her outdoor Christmas decorations. They
bundled up in heavy coats, mittens, and hats and
proceeded to follow Cora's directions about where
she liked to hang each light strand and wreath.

After an hour, things were taking shape nicely.
However, one of the steps on the ladder they'd
brought over was a bit wobbly, and as Tom worked
on a light strand above a big picture window, his foot
slipped. He tottered and almost fell, and as he caught
himself, his left foot (shod in a heavy boot) went
through the window.

Felicity gasped.

"Dad! You okay?" shouted Jake.

"Yes!" Tom yelled. He descended the ladder
carefully.

Turning to his wife, he muttered, "What a mess." He shook his head in frustration.

"It was an accident," Felicity replied. "I'm just glad you didn't hurt yourself."

Tom reached into his pocket for his cell phone. "I'll call Jim," he said. Their friend owned a local glass company.

After a couple of minutes, Tom hung up his phone and shook his head again, this time in wonder.

"What is it?" Felicity asked.

"Jim is going to give us the repair for free. He loved that we were doing this for Cora and said everyone should help their neighbors out more."

Finn and Jake gave each other a high five. "It's like you always say, Mom!" Finn exclaimed. "Giving *is* contagious!"

Father God, You have blessed me much more than I deserve. Help me to give out of that abundance this year, instead of bemoaning what I don't have. Thank You for the gift of Jesus—the gift that set us right with You; the gift that cost You everything and provided for us beyond our wildest imaginings. In Your generosity, You paved the way for us to be scandalously, ridiculously generous.

But who am I, and what is my people, that we should be able to offer so willingly after this sort? for all things come of thee, and of thine own have we given thee.
1 CHRONICLES 29:14 KJV

10 Ways to Bless Others This Christmas:

1. Help neighbors hang their outdoor decorations.
2. Give a little bit of change every time you see an opportunity to donate to charity.
3. Go through your closets and donate extra or outgrown clothing (especially warm clothes) to a local shelter or mission.
4. Babysit for a young couple so they can Christmas shop together.
5. Give homemade bread to someone who is struggling and include the recipe, along with some encouraging Bible verses about the Bread of Life.
6. Give Christmas ornaments to newlyweds. (They usually don't have their own decorations yet.)
7. Fill a shoebox for Samaritan's Purse "Operation Christmas Child."[1]
8. Give a compliment to your church's pastor or music minister.
9. Give your child your undivided attention an hour before bedtime. Read a Christmas book together and cuddle.

10. Collect gloves, scarves, and hats. Wrap them up and drive around an area where homeless folks gather. Hand these care packages to anyone who looks like they need them.

············ 5 ············

Love

And now abide faith, hope, love, these three;
but the greatest of these is love.
1 Corinthians 13:13 nkjv

Love

*The Father has loved us so much that we are called
children of God. And we really are his children.*
1 JOHN 3:1 NCV

Sherry sat in a coffee shop with her friend and mentor, Marla. Sherry's Christmas wedding was a couple
of weeks away, and as she nursed a peppermint mocha,
she asked Marla, "Marriage is such a big commitment.
I'm so nervous! How do I know if we'll make it?"

Marla took Sherry's hand and squeezed it. She'd
been married twenty years to Dave. "I can understand you being nervous. Even marriage between
two believers is difficult and isn't always fun. There
are days I really don't like Dave, but I still act in
loving ways."

Sherry's eyebrows shot up. "You fake it?"

Marla shook her head. "No, not really. At times,
love comes naturally. Other days, we choose love.
It's a constant death to self, just like parenting or"—
she smiled—"friendship. We choose the way of
self-sacrifice instead of our own comfort. When we

do that, God gives us peace, endurance, and grows a deeper love in us for that person."

"Sounds so hard!" Sherry said, sighing.

"It is. . .but it's also wonderful. The best things in life don't come easily," Marla said. "Sherry, think of how God loves us. He chose to send Jesus into the world. He knew that that road would ultimately lead to Jesus' betrayal and death. But He loved us too much to turn His back. When we love as God loves, we give ourselves as a gift to Him and others, and He makes something beautiful of it."

Lord, thank You for choosing the way of self-sacrifice instead of comfort when You sent Jesus as that very first Christmas present. Thank You for the ways He was present with others. He showed us the way to boldly love even those who've been deemed "unlovable." Give me the strength to die to myself daily in my relationships so others see You living through me. As I shop, cook, travel, and spend time with family and friends this holiday season, give me patience and compassion. May I be present with them to listen, learn—and love.

Surely your goodness and love will follow me all the days of my life, and I will dwell in the house of the LORD forever.
PSALM 23:6 NIV

10 Ways to Bless Others this Christmas:

1. Adopt a housing project with your church or small group. Bring a holiday feast to them, and provide games for the children.
2. Serve a meal at a local soup kitchen.
3. Call someone you've been meaning to get in touch with just to talk.
4. Do a chore for a family member—preferably a task they dread.
5. Shop for gifts for an elderly friend to give to family and friends.
6. Write a love letter to Jesus on your Facebook page.
7. When you pay for your meal at the drive-through, pay for someone behind you.
8. Give an extra-nice tip to your hairdresser or restaurant server.
9. Do family devotions around the Christmas tree each night of Advent.
10. Plan something small, but special, for a spouse, friend, child, or roommate on each of the twelve days leading up to Christmas.

.... **6** ....

Rejoice

Rejoice greatly, Daughter Zion! Shout,
Daughter Jerusalem! See, your king comes to you,
righteous and victorious, lowly and riding on
a donkey, on a colt, the foal of a donkey.
ZECHARIAH 9:9 NIV

Rejoice

*"For the Lord your God is living among you.
He is a mighty savior. He will take delight in you
with gladness. With his love, he will calm all your
fears. He will rejoice over you with joyful songs."*
Zephaniah 3:17 nlt

Did you know there are over 200 verses in the Bible
containing the word "rejoice"? Some passages urge
us to rejoice over God's works and His gifts; others
command us to rejoice always, even in hard times.

Rejoicing is a habit which draws us closer to
the heart of God and keeps us in tune with His
purposes. Like prayer, it's also a powerful weapon
against Satan's schemes. In 2 Chronicles 20 (kjv), the
Israelites were facing enormous odds against three
enemy armies. However, God told the Israelites
through the musician and prophet Jahaziel to
"stand ye still" and see what God would do. The
next morning, Jehosophat appointed "singers unto
the Lord" to go in front of the army and praise
their Creator. While they rejoiced in the Lord, the

Israelites' foes destroyed one another.

What a perfect picture of the power of praise! Rejoicing in God during turbulent times—those moments when hope seems like a distant memory and despair threatens to drown us—tells the devil that we won't be defeated by mere circumstance. Instead, we trust in God's character and His promises, no matter what.

One way we can develop a habit of rejoicing is to remember that regardless of what we do or don't do, our Heavenly Father delights in us and will never leave us. With His love, He calms our fears. And— get this—He sings and *rejoices over us*.

Doesn't that make you want to shout "Hallelujah!"?

God of Angel Armies, You are mighty to save. You are the same yesterday, today, and forever. I rejoice in Your works and ways. I praise You not only for who You are, but for what You do. When I am in need, You do battle for me. I don't have to fear because You are my deliverer. I don't need to worry because You are taking care of me. Thank You for living in me. Thank You for delighting in and rejoicing over me. You sing over me. . .I can hardly fathom that thought! You are so good to me.

And you shall have joy and exultant delight,
and many will rejoice over his birth.
LUKE 1:14 AMP

10 Ways to Bless Others This Christmas:

1. Host a neighborhood "carol sing/cookie exchange" in your home.
2. Coordinate a free night of candlelight Christmas worship at an outdoor pavilion or park.
3. Send a praise and worship CD to someone who's going through a hard time.
4. Before breakfast or dinner with your family or friends, take turns thanking God for five things you regularly take for granted.
5. Volunteer to ring a bell for the Salvation Army.[2]
6. Ask the next Salvation Army bell ringer you see if you can buy them a hot drink.
7. Make a CD or video of your family singing carols and send it to a long-distance family member (don't worry if you're not that musical—they'll still love it!).
8. Put together a video slideshow with music for a sick friend (you can do this for free on www.animoto.com).
9. Offer to play an instrument or sing at church during the Christmas season.
10. Buy tickets to a Christmas musical event for a family in crisis.

7

Rest

For he has somewhere spoken of the seventh day in this way: "And God rested on the seventh day from all his works"…So then, there remains a Sabbath rest for the people of God, for whoever has entered God's rest has also rested from his works as God did from his.

HEBREWS 4:4, 9–10 ESV

Rest

*God has told his people, "Here is a place of rest;
let the weary rest here. This is a place of quiet rest."
But they would not listen.*
ISAIAH 28:12 NLT

At times, our desire to have a Pinterest-worthy
Christmas overwhelms us, and we fill our calendars
with non-essential activities. We get caught up in
advertising hype, spend (and eat) more than we
should, and experience post-holiday regret. Holiday
gatherings with family turn into tense arenas of
dysfunction. Idealism fades, reality sets in—and it
isn't always pretty.

Why not try something different this year?
Put "rest" on your to-do list. In 2 Thessalonians
1:7 (KJV), Paul the apostle wrote, "And to you who
are troubled, rest with us." He was writing to the
church at Thessalonica, a place which had undergone
extreme persecution for a long period of time.

The word *rest* in this verse comes from the
Greek word *anesis*. One scholar has said that the

word was used in the secular Greek world to denote the release of a bowstring that has been under great pressure.[3]

When we are under financial, job, or relational stress, God knows that we need times of reprieve. Not only does He give us permission to rest, He gives supernatural joy when we leave our concerns in His hands.

Prune your to-do list and social calendar. Ask your family what their favorite Christmas traditions are, and shelve the rest. After all, Jesus came so that we would have abundant life. His birth doesn't give us an excuse to be frenzied.

Loosen the bow and release your expectations. The result just might be joy—and perfect peace.

Jehovah Jireh, You provide all I'll ever need. Forgive me for working too hard and thinking that everything is up to me. I know that You made me not only for work but also for rest. Help me to take time for a Sabbath, and grant me the grace to trust that when I make space for this holy pause in my week, You will take care of everything. Even You rested, Lord, on the seventh day. Thank You for that example. I praise You for the ways You care for me, so intimately and personally. Amen.

"But now the LORD my God has given me rest on every side; there is neither adversary nor misfortune."
1 KINGS 5:4 NASB

10 Ways to Bless Others This Christmas:

1. Model a sane Christmas schedule and budget for others.
2. Clean someone's house as your Christmas gift to them.
3. Offer to babysit overnight for a friend with a new baby; let the parents sleep while you take care of feedings and diaper changes.
4. Plan a few nights at home with the family during Advent. Pretend the electricity is out and do everything—eat, play cards or games, talk—by candlelight.
5. Go grocery shopping for an elderly church member.
6. Make a meal for someone recuperating from an illness or surgery.
7. Let someone nap while you clean up the Christmas dinner they prepared.
8. Collect pajamas for a local women's shelter.
9. Carry someone's packages out to their car when you're at the mall.
10. Buy restaurant gift cards and randomly present them to people shopping in the same store as you.

8

Comfort

He comforts us in all our troubles so that we can comfort others. When they are troubled, we will be able to give them the same comfort God has given us.
2 CORINTHIANS 1:4 NLT

Comfort

*In the multitude of my thoughts within
me thy comforts delight my soul.*
PSALM 94:19 KJV

When the angels spoke to the shepherds, they declared:
"Glory to God in the highest [heaven], and on earth
peace among men with whom He is well pleased [men
of goodwill, of His favor]" (Luke 2:14 AMP).

Why did they say *this*? Maybe they knew that
when we think about God, we are often ashamed
of our weaknesses, trapped by our insecurities, and
deathly afraid we'll never be accepted. Perhaps the
angels were reassuring the shepherds—lower-class,
smelly laborers—that it was okay to approach *this*
Messiah. . .because they had already pleased God.

Can you accept the truth that He loves you
beyond what you can ever imagine? Can you rest
in His approval and place your identity squarely
on His shoulders, not on your appearance or
accomplishments? If you can, it will change your life.

When you feel comforted by such a glorious

truth, you can then comfort others. When you know—all the way to the tips of your toes—that He delights in you, it changes the way you think, believe, and act.

"In the life, death, and resurrection of Jesus— our Heroic Prince of Peace—our lives have become a function of the One whom the Father loves. Received by God through Christ, you and I—those who are undeniably beloved by the Father—simply cannot be abandoned or forsaken."[4]

We are beloved. It's one of the greatest gifts of that first Christmas.

Holy Father, You called Your Son "beloved." You delight in me as You delight in Jesus. I can hardly comprehend the thought that I can do nothing to earn Your love. Thank You for loving me far beyond what I can understand. I pray for my eyes to be opened to the fact of my beloved-ness, so I can share Your truth with others. As the shepherds ran from their hills and animals to behold Your glory, I will run from worldly treasures and pleasures so I can come close to You. By my excitement over Your promises, may I bring others with me to eternal glory.

Comfort, comfort my people, says your God. Speak tenderly to Jerusalem, and cry to her that her warfare is ended, that her iniquity is pardoned, that she has received from the LORD's hand double for all her sins.
ISAIAH 40:1–2 ESV

10 Ways to Bless Others This Christmas:

1. Wear a dress every day in December to participate in Dressember,[5] a movement that benefits International Justice Mission. IJM is an organization that rescues slaves and prosecutes human traffickers.
2. Find a hospice organization to volunteer with during the holidays.
3. Buy someone a ticket to a Christmas movie, and go with them.
4. Take your kids or grandkids to a drive-through Nativity presentation.
5. Volunteer with the Make-a-Wish Foundation.[6]
6. Give used or gently-used baby clothes and furniture to a crisis pregnancy center.
7. Sit with someone who's hurting. Hold their hand if it's comfortable for them and for you.
8. Call a Ronald McDonald House[7] and ask how you can serve their residents.
9. Take baked goods to the nurses' station at a nearby hospital on Christmas Day.
10. Get together with friends and plan a "Christmas Carol Flash Mob" at a public place.

Shine

"In the same way, let your good deeds shine out for all to see, so that everyone will praise your heavenly Father."
MATTHEW 5:16 NLT

Shine

*The people that walked in darkness have seen
a great light: they that dwell in the land of the
shadow of death, upon them hath the light shined.*
ISAIAH 9:2 KJV

"Good King Wenceslas looked out on the Feast of
Stephen/When the snow lay round about, deep and
crisp and even. . .You who will bless the poor shall
yourselves find blessing."

Do you know the story behind the Christmas
carol "Good King Wenceslas"? In the mid-1800s,
prolific Anglican minister and musician John Neale
wrote the words, and set them to an old Swedish
tune, to honor a Bohemian Duke named Wenceslas
for his charitable works.

After Wenceslas' father died, the eighteen-year-
old took over governing what is now Czechoslovakia.
He reformed the judicial system, encouraged people
of faith to build congregations, and showed Christian
concern for those in poverty. "He reportedly cut fire-
wood for orphans and widows, often carrying the

provisions on his own shoulders through the snow."[8]

As Christ-followers, we are on a mission in the world. Just as the star over Bethlehem shone to help the three magi find the baby Jesus, we have been placed in our cities and jobs at this moment and for a specific purpose. The joy and peace He gives us, especially in the midst of difficulties, shine brightly into a world groaning with despair.

Wenceslas knew it was a disciple's duty to seek justice, minister to the poor, and carry others' burdens. When we do, people around us will be drawn to Jesus.

Conquering Christ, You promise to renew all things. I ache for that day. May I rise up as a servant-leader, shining Your light into dark corners where fear, disease, and hatred dwell. Help me not hold back, Lord, out of cowardice or uncertainty. Instead, let me surrender my fear to follow the high calling You have placed on my life. Holy Spirit, in board rooms, hospital rooms, living rooms, and prayer rooms, let believers' offerings of praise and supplication be sweet to Your ears. And as we rise from our knees, strengthen our hearts, oh gracious Lord, to be the Church.

Then Jesus spoke to them again, saying, "I am the
light of the world. He who follows Me shall
not walk in darkness, but have the light of life."
JOHN 8:12 NKJV

10 Ways to Bless Others This Christmas:

1. Collect flashlights and batteries, and give them to homeless shelters.
2. Get a group together and enter a float in a lighted Christmas parade.
3. Talk to a hospital or hospice chaplain and see how you might assist them during the Christmas season, either with prayer or more hands-on help using your gifts and talents.
4. Offer to chaperone a holiday party with your local Child Evangelism Fellowship[9] organization.
5. Help with a holiday camp at the nearest YMCA.[10]
6. Pick up trash around your neighborhood or city.
7. Paint someone's fence for them.
8. Host a "free hot chocolate" station outside your house or at a local event.
9. Sponsor a young person at your church so they can attend a holiday event they otherwise couldn't afford.
10. Pay a college student's registration fee for a winter mission trip or camp.

Listen

*The Lord GOD has given me the tongue of those who
are taught, that I may know how to sustain with a
word him who is weary. Morning by morning he
awakens; he awakens my ear to hear as those who
are taught. The Lord GOD has opened my ear,
and I was not rebellious; I turned not backward.*

ISAIAH 50:4–5 ESV

Listen

*"Listen carefully to everything I tell you.
Don't pay attention to other gods—
don't so much as mention their names."*
Exodus 23:13 MSG

Angels are prominent throughout the four Gospels'
nativity narratives. An angel came to Mary to
announce her holy pregnancy. Angels visited Joseph
three times: when he was about to divorce Mary;
after the birth (to warn him about Herod's cruel
plans and command him to take his family to
Egypt); and in Egypt, after the danger had passed.
An angel visited Zechariah to announce John the
Baptist's birth, and an angel warned the magi not to
return to Herod after they had visited the baby Jesus.

What if one (or more) of the people in the
nativity story had not listened to the angel? Suppose
Joseph had gone back to sleep after the angel woke
him up when Herod's soldiers were searching for
babies to kill. If that had happened, the results
would have been disastrous. Perhaps Heaven held

its collective breath each time an angel instructed a central character in the story.

Or, maybe God sat in peaceful silence, trusting the hearts of the people He chose to carry out His divine will. *They will obey,* He mused. *They know, love, and obey me implicitly.*

How about us? Do we take God's instructions carefully? Do we take time to sit, read the scriptures, listen to the Holy Spirit, and obey His promptings? It's hard to fathom that God could trust us with choices that have eternal consequences, but He does.

The ways Mary, Joseph, and the magi listened and obeyed blesses me, Father. Their choices changed the world! I long to be obedient, but sometimes I doubt that I can follow through. Forgive me for the times I ignore Your voice out of fear. Thank You for believing in me more than I believe in myself. I praise You for the gift of the Holy Spirit, who helps me know what to say and do. Thank You for the boldness and wisdom You give me. May my heart be courageous and my ears be tuned in to Your instructions.

The Lord came and stood there and called as he had before, "Samuel, Samuel!" Samuel said, "Speak, Lord. I am your servant and I am listening."
1 Samuel 3:10 NCV

10 Ways to Bless Others This Christmas:

1. Instead of saying, "let me know what I can do" when someone goes through a loss, ask "what can I do?" Follow through quickly on their request.
2. Be patient with someone who's bereaved during the holidays. They may not want to participate as they usually do.
3. Take a treat to the person playing Santa at the mall. They have a difficult job!
4. Listen—fully—to your child, friend, or spouse. Don't interrupt, and only ask questions when they pause.
5. Be present with someone who's hurting. Don't be afraid of tears or silence.
6. Volunteer to teach ESL (English as a Second Language) at a local church or community center.
7. Talk to a local restaurant owner and see if you can collect their unused goods and transport them to a food pantry.
8. Ask an elderly family member questions about their past. Record their answers.

9. Collect simple, tasty family recipes and give them to a college-age relative or friend.
10. With permission, plant an evergreen tree in the front yard of someone who's lost a child, in the child's honor.

Be Content

*I know how to live on almost nothing or with
everything. I have learned the secret of living
in every situation, whether it is with a full
stomach or empty, with plenty or little.*

PHILIPPIANS 4:12 NLT

Be Content

*"You're blessed when you're content with just
who you are—no more, no less. That's the
moment you find yourselves proud owners
of everything that can't be bought."*
MATTHEW 5:5 MSG

In 2003, newly-single Mark had a job, but it barely
paid his bills. That year, he made stocking-stuffer gifts
for his three kids, spent his small Christmas bonus
on one large present for each child, and sent his close
relatives long, hand-written letters. He turned down
most of the social invitations he received to save
money, time, and gas. At first, he felt sad about the
necessary changes he'd made.

However, something happened as the December
days slowly passed: He and the kids rediscovered the
simple pleasures of the season. They baked cookies
while listening to Christmas music. Mark unpacked
once-forgotten books and movies, and the family
spent many hours cuddled together on the couch. "I
like this Christmas," his seven-year-old, Thomas, said
one night.

"Me, too," Mark replied.

Friends, are we complaining because God has us in a place we don't like? Are we praying for contentment in the midst of difficulty? Or are we begging God to change our circumstances?

Instead of groaning and fretting, let's say "no" to senseless busyness and carve out time to ponder the Lord's works and ways. When we look into His face, He fills us with wonder, gratitude, and peace. We can then pass on those attributes to others in our circles. What a gift! We also become willing to sacrifice for the Lord because He has given so much to us.

Contentment isn't easy to come by, especially during weeks of conspicuous consumption. However, it *is* possible—with God's help.

Heavenly Father, You know this season challenges me. Advertising lures me away from contentment and towards dissatisfaction. Forgive me for lust, greed, and selfish ambition. I want to seek after eternal, not temporary, treasures. Help me be like Paul the Apostle, who wrote that he was content whether "well fed or hungry." Whether I have much or little, Lord, I thank You for the daily bread You supply. Forgive me for the times I have taken Your blessings for granted. Let me hold them loosely. I pray that I will become a disciple known for gracious living and giving.

But I am calm and quiet, like a
baby with its mother. I am at peace. . .
PSALM 131:2 NCV

Ten Ways to Bless Others at Christmas:

1. Serve at a soup kitchen.
2. Take lunch to your child at school—just because.
3. Invite your spouse out on a date. Better yet, "kidnap" him or her overnight.
4. Plan a weekly "at home" night during Advent—make soup and homemade bread, light a fire in the fireplace, and play board games. Invite one other family to join you each week.
5. Make a homemade gift for someone this year. (No perfectionism allowed!)
6. Pay for a restaurant meal for a firefighter, police officer, or member of the military.
7. If you live in a snowy climate, shovel a neighbor's walk and driveway.
8. Send Christmas cards to the nearest veterans' hospital, telling them "thank you" for their service.
9. Provide a meal for Habitat for Humanity[11] construction workers.
10. Help construct a Habitat home.

················ 12 ················

Praise

*The shepherds went back, glorifying and
praising God for all that they had heard
and seen, just as had been told them.*
LUKE 2:20 NASB

Praise

He is the one you praise; he is your God,
who performed for you those great and
awesome wonders you saw with your own eyes.
Deuteronomy 10:21 niv

Anna was the New Testament's only named prophetess. Luke describes her as a widow—only married seven years before losing her husband—and a fixture at the temple. Anna worshipped day and night, fasting and praying. For decades after her husband's death had left her alone, Anna hadn't grieved without hope or relied on the charity of others to keep her going. Instead, she clung tight to God, serving Him at the temple.

When Mary and Joseph came with the baby Jesus to His purification ceremony, Anna—along with Simeon, a priest—realized that she was beholding the Messiah. How did she know? The years spent in God's holy presence had given her an intimacy with Him. She heard His voice and knew His truth.

In fact, after she saw the baby Jesus, she began to speak about the child to all who were looking for the redemption of Jerusalem (Luke 2:38). Anna became one of the first Christian missionaries!

God longs for us to spend time at the feet of Jesus, worshipping. We need this time (especially during the hectic weeks leading up to and during the holidays) to correct our perspective and reorder our priorities. Without worship and praise, our minds become polluted by the world, and we simply cannot make godly decisions. However, when we know His voice, we can obey Him and share His love with those around us.

Make time this season to worship your King. You won't regret it.

Almighty King, thank You for coming as a baby to redeem the world from sin. Thank You for Your forgiveness and mercy. Forgive me for the times I am too busy to meditate on Your goodness. Forgive me for the moments I haven't spent worshipping and listening. Quiet my heart, Jesus. Speak Your truth to me. I want to know You better and make You known to those who desperately need Your saving grace. During this busy season, help me to find—and create—spaces of time to sit with You. I love You, precious Lord.

At the very time Simeon was praying, [Anna] showed up, broke into an anthem of praise to God, and talked about the child to all who were waiting expectantly for the freeing of Jerusalem.
LUKE 2:38 MSG

10 Ways to Bless Others this Christmas:

1. Invite women in your neighborhood to a Christmas tea in your home. During the meal, spend a few minutes praising God for what He's done for you.
2. Bring an unchurched friend to the Christmas Eve service at your congregation.
3. Thank the store manager the next time you hear Christian music while shopping.
4. Buy flowers for a single person.
5. Put a Jesus-themed decoration on your front lawn.
6. Invite people to drop by (no gifts necessary) for a "finger foods" open house one night during Advent. Make it simple and festive.
7. Give your testimony at a local Celebrate Recovery[12] meeting.
8. Take an ill friend to look at Christmas lights.
9. Make coupon books full of fun, low-cost activities to put in your family members' stockings.
10. Eat out less; eat in more. Take the money you've saved and buy a cow or pig through World Vision[13].

--------- 13 ---------

Gather

Save us, O God of our salvation; gather us together and deliver us from the nations, that we may give thanks to Your holy name and glory in Your praise.
1 Chronicles 16:35 amp

Gather

"Nor shall you glean your vineyard, nor shall you gather the fallen fruit of your vineyard; you shall leave them for the needy and for the stranger. I am the LORD your God."
LEVITICUS 19:10 NASB

One summer, Barbara's father told her mother to "get out or else." She says because God—and their mother—took care of them, she and her siblings never felt poor. They gathered their courage, worked hard, and did whatever they needed to in order to survive. However, when the holidays came, the family knew that presents, clothes, and food would be sparse.

"One afternoon, I walked home from school and discovered a large box on our front porch. . . After we all got home, Mother opened it. Inside were nice clothes for my sister and me. . .we tried on the beautiful clothes and were happily outfitted for parties and church. We felt truly grateful for being remembered."

Also, she says, "The first holiday in Baton Rouge,

each elementary class gathered canned goods for needy families. When my ten-year-old brother's teacher asked if anyone in his class knew of someone who needed help, he told her we did. In our previous town, we had helped deliver boxes of food to needy families for years. Now it became our turn to graciously accept one. At that time in our lives, it was truly a gift we needed."

What have you received from the Lord? Food, shelter, job, clothes? Why not share your abundance with others this season? You might be the very person who brings hope and joy to an otherwise hopeless situation. Who knows? You might be the recipient of such kindness one day.8

What can I bring You, Lord, that You don't have already? What do I have that You haven't given me? I lay everything at Your feet as an offering, Father. Most Holy One, lead me to the people who need the light of Your presence this Christmas. May I be a servant who reflects Your mercy and love, a servant whose light is but a reflection of Your glory. I pray that people will be drawn to Your light in me, and not my own personality or attributes. To You be the glory, forever and ever, amen.

*"Behold, at that time I will deal with all who afflict you;
I will save the lame, and gather those who were
driven out; I will appoint them for praise and fame
in every land where they were put to shame."*
ZEPHANIAH 3:19 NKJV

10 Ways to Bless Others This Christmas:

1. Pray for people on the highway, subway, or metro as you come and go from work or shopping.
2. Read *Advent and Christmas Wisdom from G. K. Chesterton* by Thom Satterlee. This series of daily reflections ends with practical steps to allow the Good News to impact your schedule.
3. Fast from one meal each week this season. Use the time to pray for coworkers, family members, or friends.[14]
4. Gather shoes for orphans as a workplace or small group.[15]
5. Gather books and donate them to a local community center.
6. Gather coats for children in need.[16]
7. Gather friends and start a Hope for Justice Group for Abolition International.[17]
8. Gather extra funds and pay off someone's layaway bill, anonymously.
9. Gather a "Fix-it" team. Can you or your friends fix cars or do home repairs? Help a single mom with a "honey-do" list.

10. Gather to pray: Join the Presidential Prayer Team[18] and regularly share the requests—for our nation, leaders, and troops—with your loved ones at mealtimes.

14

Remember

LORD, remember my suffering and my misery,
my sorrow and trouble. Please remember me and
think about me. But I have hope when I think of this:
The LORD's love never ends; his mercies never stop.
They are new every morning; LORD, your loyalty is great.
I say to myself, "The LORD is mine, so I hope in him."
The LORD is good to those who hope in him, to those who
seek him. It is good to wait quietly for the LORD to save.

LAMENTATIONS 3:19–26 NCV

Remember

Once again I'll go over what GOD has done,
lay out on the table the ancient wonders;
I'll ponder all the things you've accomplished,
and give a long, loving look at your acts.
PSALM 77:11–12 MSG

After Mary gave birth to Jesus, scriptures give us
a glimpse of her mixed emotions. The Gospel of
Luke (NLT) uses these words to describe her state
of mind: confused, disturbed, thoughtful, amazed,
frantic.[19] And what did she think when Simeon the
priest prophesied over the baby that "a sword will
pierce your very soul" (Luke 2:35 NLT)? Those are not
exactly the words a new mom hopes for!

Writer Nancy Franson[20] says,

She who was highly favored received the gift of
bearing the Son of God Most High. But this one
who was highly favored was also chosen to stand
at the foot of the cross and watch her son die a
horrific death. That's what it cost her to be God's

handmaiden. Somehow, that thought gave me comfort as I thought about the many of us who are watching dear ones struggle. Being chosen as an instrument of blessing doesn't come without cost. But this we remember: God is with us. Emmanuel!

When we accept Christ as our Savior, we have to remember that our faith comes with a price. We are no longer free to do as we please; instead, we give up our rights in order to serve the living King. Of course, what we receive in return is priceless.

God is, indeed, with us every second of every minute of our lives. No matter what we feel, or what we go through, we can remember that His comfort and peace is ours for the asking.

When a sword pierces my soul—due to abandonment, betrayal, or abuse—be my comfort, sweet Jesus. As You chose Mary to be highly favored, You have gifted me with Your forgiveness. Help me to remember that You will never leave my side, even when I feel that all hope is lost. Thank You for the promise that God is with *me*—my Emmanuel. You are *my* Mighty King, Prince of Peace, and Wonderful Counselor. I praise You for the ways You show yourself to be all those things in my sometimes muddled, mixed-up mind and spirit.

I pray that the LORD our God will remember my prayer day and night. May he help everyone in Israel each day, in whatever way we need it.
1 KINGS 8:59 CEV

10 Ways to Bless Others This Christmas:

1. Remember those who have died by setting up a memorial tree in your church's foyer. Have congregants bring a cross labeled with their loved one's name to hang on the tree.

2. Remember how God has saved you. Write out your testimony and pray for an opportunity to share it with someone this season.

3. Remember families with young children. Help your church plan an interactive family Christmas Eve service. Hold it earlier in the evening than your normal Christmas Eve service.

4. Remember the hungry. Donate to a local food bank.

5. Remember prisoners. Find a small Christmas ornament or gift on CBD.com and order a case or two to be sent to your local prison (check with them first).

6. Remember those in the military. Donate calling cards so they can call home.

7. Remember the works of the Lord. Before opening gifts, talk about the answers to prayer

you've received over the last year.

8. Remember orphans. Collect shoes for Buckner International.[21]

9. Remember widows. invite a widow to your home for dinner during the Christmas season.

10. Remember those who work on Christmas Day. If you're traveling, bring candy canes (with hand-written or typed scriptures attached) to hand out to airport, train, bus, or shuttle employees.

····· 15 ·····

Be Humble

*At that time the disciples came to Jesus and asked,
"Who, then, is the greatest in the kingdom of heaven?"
He called a little child to him, and placed the child among
them. And he said: "Truly I tell you, unless you change and
become like little children, you will never enter the kingdom
of heaven. Therefore, whoever takes the lowly position of
this child is the greatest in the kingdom of heaven."*

MATTHEW 18:1–4 NIV

Be Humble

The fear of the LORD is the instruction of wisdom;
and before honour is humility.
PROVERBS 15:33 KJV

Mary is a model of biblical humility. When Gabriel came to her with the shocking news that she had been chosen to bear the Messiah, surely she questioned the timing of such unexpected news—but she didn't say, "Now, wait a minute, this isn't the way I had pictured things. I don't want a baby right now. I'm too young!" Rather, she trusted God and responded in humility and obedience.

After learning she was pregnant, Mary almost immediately went to stay with Elizabeth, her cousin, who was miraculously expecting a baby, too. Perhaps God didn't only want them to have bonding time. Maybe He wanted Mary to be nurtured and prepared for what lay ahead, by walking through such a transformative experience with a godly mentor. Under Elizabeth's tutelage, Mary began to grow into the mother Jesus would need.

Mary's humility allowed her not only to trust God with her future but also to seek counsel from someone older and wiser. When we can receive advice from others, we position ourselves to grow in maturity and wisdom.

We live in a very independent culture. Realize that it's okay to ask for help when you need it!

What are you lacking this Christmas (financial stability, peace, guidance)? Don't be afraid; ask for help, and offer assistance when it's needed and desired. When we develop a humble heart, we can trust God, obey even His most audacious requests, and shine for Him.

Father God, I am so impressed that Mary humbly bowed her head and received the angel's news with obedience and praise. I want to be like her—humble, servant-hearted, and thankful. May I be a person who is willing to take both criticism and guidance with grace. Give me the strength and courage to obey You in every detail of my life.

Therefore, as the elect of God, holy and beloved, put on tender mercies, kindness, humility, meekness, longsuffering. . .
COLOSSIANS 3:12 NKJV

10 Ways to Bless Others This Christmas:

1. Brag on other people—preferably in front of them.
2. Champion your peers' successes on social media.
3. Fast from spending money on yourself during the holidays.
4. Ask someone wise for help with a problem.
5. Ask your spouse for their input the next time you need to make a decision.
6. Become a mentor for young women or men in transitional phases of life through Christian Women's Job Corps or Christian Men's Job Corps.[22]
7. Offer to be a substitute Bible study teacher or nursery worker during the holidays, when people are often traveling and church staff members scramble to find volunteers.
8. Give a plate of goodies to your child's music teacher or sports coach.
9. Ask children to bake with you and let them sample the batter.
10. Buy toys on discount throughout the year, and give them to Toys for Tots.[23]

16

Inspire

*And when they were come into the house,
they saw the young child with Mary his mother,
and fell down, and worshipped him: and when
they had opened their treasures, they presented unto
him gifts; gold, and frankincense and myrrh.*
MATTHEW 2:11 KJV

Inspire

Bravo, GOD, Bravo! Everyone join in
the great shout: Encore! In awe before
the beauty, in awe before the might.
PSALM 96:7 MSG

What inspires you about the Christmas season? For
Darlene, it's "the simple beauty found in nature.
God's attention to detail is astonishing!"

Cassandra says the "smells" of Christmas (ginger-
bread, pine, etc.) inspire her.

Dan, a music minister, is inspired by "the music
and words of worship. They serve as tools to unify us
under the banner of God's love, faithfulness, blessing,
guidance, and mission."

Maybe it's a person who inspires you. Jill relates,
"All the widows or widowers that I get to see over
the Christmas season inspire me. This is a difficult
time of year, but they are still smiling and laughing!
They have no idea how much this encourages me,
to be thankful for my spouse and for each day God
gives me."

Emily explains, "I'm inspired by the strength of our elders. My ninety-six-year-old grandmother is the hardest working lady I know. She inspires me to work harder. My father-in-law tells amazing stories of his childhood. It's a miracle many times over that he's alive today at the age of 99. Getting to be around them at this time of year is such a blessing. I appreciate each holiday I get to spend with them, more and more as the years pass. I haven't heard nearly enough of their stories yet!"

Let's pray that we would be an inspiration to others. We have the Answer to the world's problems, and Christmas is the perfect time to share it in winsome ways.

Heavenly Father, so many things about this season inspire me. I love the stories of Mary and Joseph, the wise men and the shepherds, and Elizabeth and Zachariah. I love the symbolism of candles and gifts, the lights on houses and trees, and the music I hear everywhere. I love the way You dropped into our world quietly and gently, as a child dependent on humans for everything. I love the sounds of children's laughter and the sight of Christmas pageants. Help me to spread the story of Jesus, not just at Christmastime, but all year-round.

"Blessed be the Lord God of Israel, for He has visited us and accomplished redemption for His people, and has raised up a horn of salvation for us in the house of David His servant— as He spoke by the mouth of His holy prophets from of old."
LUKE 1:68–70 NASB

10 Ways to Bless Others This Christmas:

1. Frame an inspiring quote or photo and give it as a gift to someone special.
2. Buy a family member a membership to a museum.
3. Take a child to a planetarium.
4. Make crafts from nature and give them away to friends.
5. Decorate an outdoor tree with birdseed-and-peanut butter ornaments.
6. Write and address a handwritten thank-you note to an author or speaker who's blessed you, and send it via their publisher or agent.
7. Write a letter to the editor of a local or online paper or magazine about something you read that inspired you.
8. Help with costumes or technical support for a Christmas pageant.
9. Go to a children's musical production. . .and clap/cheer wildly for them.
10. Hang mistletoe or a kissing ball in your home. Stand under it regularly with someone you love.

----------- 17 -----------

Forgive

"But if you do not forgive men their trespasses,
neither will your Father forgive your trespasses."
MATTHEW 6:15 NKJV

Forgive

"Hear my prayers and the prayers of your people Israel when we pray facing this place. Hear from your home in heaven, and when you hear, forgive us."
1 Kings 8:30 NCV

During the holidays, we often spend time with people who've hurt us. How do we move on—forgive, let go, and perhaps even find a restored relationship—when our friends or family members have deeply wounded us?

We can't control others' behavior, but we *can* make changes in our own lives.

Here are some practical principles:

1) *Set healthy boundaries.* Leave damaging patterns behind, as much as it depends on you, and establish new patterns. Don't enable bad behavior, and protect yourself. If it's possible, try to establish a relationship based on healthier forms of communication.

2) *Begin again.* Grieve the past, but also determine that you will not dwell there. If you can, find out about your loved one's past in order to understand his or her choices and actions. When we can empathize or have compassion for the wounds others have experienced, it can give us perspective and soften our hearts.

3) *Realize our Heavenly Father is the only perfect person.* Just as we make mistakes, our family members and friends make mistakes, too. God, through Jesus, imparted grace to us when we were at our most sinful, and He enables us to give that grace to others. He can give us the understanding, forgiveness, and strength to move forward.

Keep seeking Him and falling on His mercy. Live in the light of His love, and pray for those who have wounded you. Remember that He has forgiven you—and with His help, you can forgive, too.

Merciful Jesus, You have forgiven me much. Grant me the courage to walk in forgiveness. Help me to see others as You see them, knowing that hurting people hurt people. Continue to heal me of the deep wounds I carry so that I can grow in my faith and not get stuck in painful moments from my past. Holy Spirit, guide me as I seek to build healthy and godly relationships. I pray that I will be an example of a wounded healer—just as Jesus was.

To the Lord our God belong mercy and loving-kindness and forgiveness, for we have rebelled against Him.
DANIEL 9:9 AMP

10 Ways to Bless Others This Christmas:

1. Visit a juvenile detention center and bring gifts.
2. Serve on a prison ministry team.
3. Pray for those who've wronged you.
4. Send a Christmas card to someone you are struggling to forgive.
5. Write down verses about grace and mercy, and then place them where people gather—on library shelves, store displays, etc.
6. Start a chain love letter for someone going through a hard time.
7. Make a paper chain of Old Testament prophecies that Jesus fulfilled and read one as a family each night before bed.
8. Go through your Christmas decorations and give some away to a thrift shop connected to charity.
9. Pool the money you would spend on gifts at the office and make a donation to a favorite non-profit organization or ministry.
10. Forgive yourself for the things you've done wrong. When you do, you'll be a better friend, parent, and spouse.

······· **18** ·······

Share

"Is it not to share your bread with the hungry, and that you bring to your house the poor who are cast out; when you see the naked, that you cover him, and not hide yourself from your own flesh?"
ISAIAH 58:7 NKJV

Share

Tell them to use their money to do good. They should be rich in good works and generous to those in need, always being ready to share with others.
1 Timothy 6:18 nlt

In the film version of *Little Women* starring Winona Ryder, the poor-but-happy March sisters Jo, Amy, and Meg sit down to a Christmas breakfast of delicacies reserved for holidays. However, after hearing from their sister Beth that a neighbor woman has children with nothing to eat, they decide to share the little they have with the family in need. Their mother ("Marmie") has taught them from infancy the biblical virtue of sacrifice.

In stark contrast, in the play *A Christmas Carol*, Ebeneezer Scrooge hates Christmas and makes everyone around him miserable with his complaints and selfishness. He loves money more than people, can't stand the thought of generosity, and loathes closing the office, even if just one day a year.

Over the course of one eventful night, Scrooge is

taught what really matters, and he changes his ways. He learns to see others through more compassionate eyes, and forgives himself for his horrid past.

Our sinful hearts often veer between the two extremes: Beth, who knew wealth is more than riches and was willing to share what little she had with someone in need, and Scrooge, who held tightly to his money because he was insecure and greedy. This Christmas, let's resolve to hold loosely to the earthly treasures God has gifted us with, and share freely.

When we share, we model the abundant love He has shown us in Jesus' birth, death, and resurrection. In doing so, we draw others closer to the Light that overcame—and is still overcoming—the world's darkness.

Precious Lord, You have shared Your very
being with us. I praise You and thank You
for Your faithfulness. Forgive me for the ways
I've been selfish and greedy. Help me become
more like You with each day that passes.
I want to be like the March sisters, not Scrooge.
Give me a generous spirit.

And do not neglect doing good and sharing,
for with such sacrifices God is pleased.
HEBREWS 13:16 NASB

10 Ways to Bless Others This Christmas:

1. Share your home. Invite a person or family in need to spend Christmas with you.
2. Share your car. Become part of a "rideshare" program.[24]
3. Share your tools as part of a tool lending library.[25]
4. Share your gifts and talents. Talk to a volunteer coordinator at your church about getting involved.
5. Share your faith. Take an evangelism training course.
6. Share your wealth. Open a charitable annuity (talk to a financial advisor you know about this).
7. Share your table. Have each person in your family invite a special teacher or mentor to a Christmas week brunch in their honor.
8. Share your books. Make a little free library for your front lawn.[26]
9. Share the love. Hire a housecleaner for a month (or three) for new parents or a single parent.
10. Share the joy. Do twelve days of good deeds leading up to Christmas Day.

·········· 19 ··········

Hope

*"I know what I am planning for you," says the L*ORD.
"I have good plans for you, not plans to hurt you.
I will give you hope and a good future."
JEREMIAH 29:11 NCV

Hope

I wait in hope for your salvation, GOD.
GENESIS 49:18 MSG

We often want immediate resolutions to our issues.
We long for God to press the "fix-it" button and
send enough money to erase all our debts. We want
physical or emotional healing but don't want to work
for it. And when He makes us wait, we falter and
begin to lose hope.

Sometimes, the Father cries "Enough!" and
answers our desperate pleas for deliverance. For
instance, He told Joseph in a dream to leave the
place where he and Mary were staying with the baby
Jesus. At other times, though, He doles out daily—
even minute-by-minute—grace.

Why does God tarry when He could snap His
celestial fingers and fix our problems in a second?
He's powerful enough, after all.

For one thing, He knows our nature. If He
answered all our prayers and we never had a
need—physical, emotional, financial—we would get

complacent. (Think about the Israelites—God parted the Red Sea and freed them from slavery, and still they rebelled. They doubted and complained. That's why He gave them manna, which would rot if they tried to store it overnight. He wanted them to trust Him for their every breath.)

At all times, friends, *He* is our miracle. God sent Jesus into the world that first Christmas to be our living water and our bread of life. He strengthens our weary hearts and supplies us with living hope. . . second by second, minute by minute, hour by hour, and day by day.

Sustainer of the world, I am tired. My heart is heavy; I've been waiting so long. Sometimes, I start to question whether You're really "for" me. Forgive me for doubting You, O Holy One. Forgive me for not trusting Your timing and Your promises. Give me strength and hope to move forward, knowing that Your plans and purposes will prevail. Give me Kingdom eyes and an eternal perspective. Shift my focus off myself and onto You. Thank You for the future You've planned for me, one full of healing and hope.

The Lord is there to rescue all who are discouraged and have given up hope.
PSALM 34:18 CEV

10 Ways to Bless Others This Christmas:

1. Have a shoe-cutting party for Sole Hope.[27]
2. Have a jewelry party for ViBella Jewelry[28] (proceeds go to Haitian craftswomen).
3. Make Christmas crafts with your kids and sell them to raise money for missions.
4. Teach someone a skill as your gift to him or her.
5. Pay someone's utility bill.
6. The next time you're in the express line at the grocery store, pay for the person behind you.
7. Give blood at a local blood bank. They often run low during the holidays.
8. Offer to pet- and/or house-sit (no charge) for a friend while they're traveling.
9. Take your children or grandchildren to an animal shelter and play with the puppies or kitties.
10. Welcome an international student into your home for Christmas dinner.

Sing

*In the same region there were some shepherds staying out
in the fields and keeping watch over their flock by night.
And an angel of the Lord suddenly stood before them,
and the glory of the Lord shone around them; and they
were terribly frightened. But the angel said to them,
"Do not be afraid; for behold, I bring you good news of
great joy which will be for all the people; for today in
the city of David there has been born for you a Savior,
who is Christ the Lord. This will be a sign for you:
you will find a baby wrapped in cloths and lying in a
manger." And suddenly there appeared with the angel
a multitude of the heavenly host praising God.*
LUKE 2:8–13 NASB

Sing

Sing to the LORD a new song; sing to the LORD,
all the earth. Sing to the LORD and praise his name;
every day tell how he saves us. Tell the nations of his
glory; tell all peoples the miracles he does, because the
LORD is great; he should be praised at all times.
PSALM 96:1–4 NCV

Mathias, an elderly shepherd, yelled, "Josiah and
Levi, come here!"

Two young boys quit running and turned toward
Mathias. Josiah shouted, "Didn't you hear the angels?
We're going to see the baby!"

"You and Levi must stay behind. The sheep need
tending."

The look in Mathias's eyes warned Josiah to keep
quiet. He glanced at Levi and muttered, "Come on.
We get the grunt work, as always."

As they walked back to Mathias, Levi motioned
to the sheep, who had been cowered into silence
by the bright lights and heavenly singing. "At least
they'll be easy to control," the boy stated.

Mathias nodded. "If they aren't, you can sing to them."

"I wanted to worship the One who has been promised!" Josiah replied.

The old man chuckled and put his hand on Josiah's shoulder. "If He's the Messiah, He'll hear your praises from here, child." He walked toward the others shepherds, who had already crested the hill and were plodding down the other side.

Levi smiled a bit. He moved to the middle of the sheep herd and said, "Josiah, could it really be so? After all this time?"

"I hope it's true. We've been waiting a long time."

"Let's sing!" Levi exclaimed. His treble voice rang out—wobbly at first, but then steadily. He sang the songs he'd learned at the temple. After a few minutes, Josiah reluctantly joined him. Soon, the boys' voices rang out strong and clear across the hill.

And in a manger, a baby smiled.

Just as the angels sang, "Glory to God in the highest," I sing to You, magnificent Lord. I praise You for providing Jesus as the Savior of the world. I praise You for using humble servants like carpenters, Jewish girls, and shepherds to put Your plan in place. Thank You for the gift of music, especially at Christmas. The familiar carols and new worship songs fill me with joy and help me put words to my feelings. I lift my voice to You, even when I can't see You. Receive my offering of praise, this season and every season.

For to us a child is born, to us a son is given,
and the government will be on his shoulders.
And he will be called Wonderful Counselor,
Mighty God, Everlasting Father, Prince of Peace.
Isaiah 9:6 niv

10 Ways to Bless Others This Christmas:

1. Play gospel-centered Christmas music at your place of business.
2. Take an elderly friend to a production of the *Hallelujah Chorus* at a local university or church.
3. Bring a youngster with you to a production of *The Nutcracker* ballet.
4. Read one story each night on the origins of different Christmas carols.
5. Play a CD of Christmas hymns around your house during the morning rush.
6. Go caroling at a hospital and offer to pray for the patients as you sing for them.
7. Are you a part of a singing, drama, or musical group? Ask a local business if you can provide free lunch-time Christmas entertainment for their patrons.
8. Post a different Christian music video each day on your Facebook feed.
9. Give a monetary gift to your local Christian radio station, or. . .
10. Help with their annual pledge drive by stuffing envelopes, manning phones, etc.

21

Compassion

The LORD passed in front of Moses, calling out, "Yahweh! The LORD! The God of compassion and mercy! I am slow to anger and filled with unfailing love and faithfulness."
EXODUS 34:6 NLT

Be Compassionate

*Finally, all [of you] should be of one and the same mind
(united in spirit), sympathizing [with one another],
loving [each other] as brethren [of one household],
compassionate and courteous (tenderhearted and humble).*

1 PETER 3:8 AMP

Because of God's gift of Jesus, and the gifts the magi
brought to the baby, Christmas is known as a season
of giving. But what would it look like if we had the
same spirit of charity every day of the year?

Christians are called to this kind of compassion.
In the Gospels, Jesus is often described as being
moved with *splagchnos* (compassion) towards the
lame, sick, and hurting. And "...every time Jesus
was moved with compassion, it always resulted in
a healing, deliverance, resurrection, supernatural
provision, or some other action that changed
someone's life. You see, compassion always produces
action. The force of compassion cannot leave a
person in the sad condition in which he was found;
it moves one to do something to change that other
person's situation."[29]

What has God delivered you from? How has He provided miraculously for you? The ways God has worked in your life can provide the basis of a ministry to others. Take the compassion God has given to you, and turn it into compassion for others.

Has He redeemed you from drug abuse? Train to work as a substance abuse counselor. Has God freed you from depression? Share your story with others, and give them hope. As you look at your life, you will see threads of resurrection. Ask the Father how He may want to use those threads to weave a tapestry of grace that will give glory to Him for generations to come.

Holy Father, You had compassion on Your children and sent Your only Son to this earth as a helpless infant. You have been showing me compassion my whole life. I praise You for the ways You've delivered, redeemed, and resurrected the dead places in me. Give me opportunities to share Your healing touch with others, Lord. Let me be attuned to the Holy Spirit as I go about my daily life, and may I bring the joy, peace, and hope of Christmas into others' lives by the compassion I show when they are hurting. In Jesus' precious name, amen.

And when Jesus went out He saw a great multitude; and He was moved with compassion for them, and healed their sick.
Matthew 14:14 NKJV

10 Ways to Bless Others This Christmas:

1. Volunteer at a local community garden to do off-season chores.
2. Research Christmas traditions from various cultures and incorporate one or more into your celebration.
3. In a deceased friend's name, send a donation to Gideons International[30] for their Bible distribution program.
4. Turn in your old cellphone to help a soldier overseas make calls back home.[31]
5. Begin a recycling program at your school or workplace.
6. Wash a neighbor's car.
7. Hold a free carwash in a public place...just because.
8. Give a gift to Angel Tree[32] from Prison Fellowship. The recipients are children of incarcerated men and women.
9. With a group of friends, make Chrismon[33] ornaments for your tree (or one at your church).
10. Help children make handprint crafts for their long-distance relatives.

22

Encourage

"Therefore the Lord himself will give you a sign.
Behold, the virgin shall conceive and bear a son,
and shall call his name Immanuel."

ISAIAH 7:14 ESV

Encourage

*When he came and had seen the grace of God,
he was glad, and encouraged them all that with
purpose of heart they should continue with the Lord.*
ACTS 11:23 NKJV

Jesus came to encourage, heal, and redeem. However, because we are fallen, His Church sometimes fails to do the same.

With tears streaming down her cheeks, Monica told Gwen, her new pastor's wife, "We went through a terrible time two years ago. Our oldest son was imprisoned for selling drugs—and the people at our church acted weird and awkward around us. Or they gave us verses out of context, patted our arm, and walked off. It was so hurtful!"

Gwen handed her a tissue. "I'm sorry. People are uncomfortable with pain sometimes. We think it's catching or something."

"You're right!" Monica said. "It was as if they were paralyzed and couldn't do anything but respond in a rote, unhelpful way. I'm not mad anymore, but it was really disappointing."

Gwen nodded. "People aren't trying to be mean, but when they haven't been though something, they can't empathize with brokenness. I can't say we'll be perfect here, but our motto is not to try and fix problems or people but to try and sit with folks in their pain. I will listen to you, and pray with you—if you want to do that—but mostly I'll just be available."

Monica sighed. "Thank you. I'm glad God led us here."

"I am, too," said Gwen.

Ask God to lead you to someone in need of His encouragement this Christmas, and share the eternal hope brought to us by the baby in the manger. Your presence might be the perfect present.

Lord, I've heard it said that the word *encourage* means "give courage." I want to give courage to others by listening to them and sitting with them in their pain. Help me to not give easy answers or advice, but instead open my mind and heart. Forgive me for being afraid of suffering with others, Father. Forgive me for being afraid of silence. And forgive me for being resentful, bitter, and angry when others fail to encourage me the way I want them to. I long to give grace to others, just as You have given grace upon grace to me.

And David was greatly distressed. . .
*but David encouraged himself in the L*ORD *his God.*
1 SAMUEL 30:6 KJV

10 Ways to Bless Others This Christmas:

1. Buy a box of Bibles or Christian books for distribution at the nearest prison (check with the staff there first as to whether you should follow any specific guidelines).
2. Write an encouraging message for your children or spouse on the bathroom mirror with a dry-erase marker.
3. Bring food to a local police or fire station on Christmas Day.
4. Set a turquoise table on your front lawn and begin to practice intentional hospitality.[34]
5. Have a card-writing party, and send the cards to wounded soldiers at Walter Reed Hospital.[35]
6. Become a Big Brother or Big Sister.[36]
7. As a family, church, or Bible study group, adopt a refugee family who's resettled. Show them the love of Jesus by providing gifts and a tree for their first Christmas in America.[37]
8. Volunteer for Meals on Wheels.[38]
9. Send a poinsettia to someone who lost a loved one during the last year.
10. Purchase or download an Advent devotional guide, and go through it with your family.

······· — 23 — ·······

Reflect

For as the heavens are higher than the earth,
so are My ways higher than your ways
and My thoughts than your thoughts.
ISAIAH 55:9 AMP

Reflect

*Remember the wonders he has performed,
his miracles, and the rulings he has given.*
1 CHRONICLES 16:12 NLT

When the angel Gabriel told Zachariah that he and
his wife would have a baby, Zachariah said to the
angel, "Do you expect me to believe this? I'm an old
man and my wife is an old woman" (Luke 1:18 MSG).

Because of the priest's disbelief, Gabriel reported
that Zechariah's voice would be taken from him
until the day of the baby's birth. Unable to speak
for several months, Zachariah had plenty of time to
reflect on God's timing and choices. The scriptures
say that his wife, Elizabeth, "went off by herself
for five months, relishing her pregnancy. 'So, this is
how God acts to remedy my unfortunate condition!'
she said" (Luke 1:25 MSG). Mary, too, reflected on
the unimaginable things God had promised—and
fulfilled. Luke 2:19 (MSG) says that she "kept all
these things to herself, holding them dear, deep
within herself."

God's ways are not our own. In fact, they often leave us speechless, needing time and space to process His work. Who among us would have commissioned our son, a heavenly ruler, to be born of a virgin in a cave full of animal dung?

What has God done for you—things that you didn't understand but still turned out for your good? What promises has He assured you of—but you're still waiting for their fulfillment?

Our fast-paced society doesn't allow us much room for reflection. Take time this season to be countercultural as you reflect, ponder, and pray. Give Him room and space to speak to you.

Your ways leave me breathless, Lord, and sometimes I am almost unable to verbalize how amazing You are. If I'm being honest, there are also moments when I feel confused and hurt by Your delays or denials. Help me to trust You, even when I don't understand what You're doing. Give me patience as You work Your will out in my life and the lives of those I love. I long to rest in Your goodness and grace, not fretting about things which are too difficult for me to fathom.

So remember that the LORD is the only true God,
whether in the sky above or on the earth below.
DEUTERONOMY 4:39 CEV

10 Ways to Bless Others This Christmas:

1. Make a scrapbook of pictures from Christmases past, and give it to a family member.
2. Make a dream/goal collage about future Christmases with your friends, kids, or spouse.
3. Fill a journal with stories about Christmas when you were a child.
4. Fill a blank book or create a blog with stories about God's faithfulness. Give it (or send the link) to a new Christian in your family or circle of friends.
5. Take a family picture in Christmas clothes and send it to far-away family members.
6. Make a video of your testimony and load it onto YouTube or Godtube.
7. Write a story about something God has done, and submit it to a website or magazine.
8. Paint a picture representing what God has done in your life. Frame it, and give it away as a gift.
9. Call a person who has been instrumental in your Christian development and thank them.
10. Make a donation to a charity in honor of someone who has greatly influenced you.

24

Bless

Out of his fullness we have all received
grace in place of grace already given.
JOHN 1:16 NIV

Bless

*And in thy seed shall all the nations of the earth be
blessed; because thou hast obeyed my voice.*
GENESIS 22:18 KJV

One of the things we hear about at Christmastime
is *re-gifting*. The word means to give someone
something you've been given. . .such as a sweater
you don't like. Workplaces and Bible study groups
have "White Elephant" or "Tacky Christmas" parties
where each person brings a dud of a gift. The group
plays a game where participants can steal a gift
they like—or one they find especially hideous and
hilarious—once or twice. It's all in good fun, until
you receive Aunt Matilda's moldy fruitcake.
However, what if we as believers turned the concept
upside down and saw re-gifting as a gospel-sharing
opportunity?

God has given us His Son, salvation, and eternal
life. He has given us spiritual gifts, the Holy Spirit,
and His presence. Why not re-gift those things to
a world in need? When we use the things God has

given us to bless others, we serve and magnify Him. We often talk about God's blessings in our lives, but did you know that we can bless the Lord?

Wow.

What gifts can you re-gift this year? Perhaps your father in-law needs the same gentle patience God has shown with you. Maybe your co-worker is desperate for a listening ear and loving, wise counsel, which the Father has provided you countless times. Give those gifts away, freely and graciously. In doing so, you'll be putting a smile on your Creator's face and spreading the Good News of Jesus.

What a holy privilege we've been given!

Jehovah Jireh, You are the one who provided the lamb for Moses on the mountaintop so he wouldn't have to sacrifice his only son. And You are the one who provided Your own Son to be the Lamb of the world. What a priceless gift I've been given! I can't thank You enough for Jesus' presence in my life. Help me to be bold and fearless in spreading the Good News. I want to "re-gift" Jesus' mercy and grace wherever I go. I long to make a difference and shine a light in this dark world. Help me, Holy One.

And Mary said: "My soul magnifies the Lord, and my spirit has rejoiced in God my Savior. . . For He who is mighty has done great things for me, and holy is His name."
LUKE 1:46–47, 49 NKJV

10 Ways to Bless Others This Christmas:

1. Instead of bringing a tacky gift to a Christmas exchange, bring a CD of Christmas music or an ornament representing Christ's birth.

2. When you send Christmas letters, talk more about God's faithfulness and less about your family's accomplishments over the last year.

3. Invite a co-worker who usually eats alone to go to lunch with your usual group of friends.

4. Ask your hairdresser how you can pray for him or her.

5. Send your accountant, lawyer, real estate agent, or other professional colleague a thank-you card and a small gift.

6. Make a donation to a disaster relief agency.

7. Decorate your cubicle or office with Christmas ornaments and greenery (if it's allowed). Play Christmas music when you can.

8. Pray for ways to "re-gift" Jesus' love throughout the holidays.

9. Ask folks at your workplace to pay $2 for the chance to wear jeans instead of dress clothes and give the money to an agreed-upon good cause.[39]

10. Set a goal to compliment others every day during the season. Before long, it will be a habit![40]

·············· 25 ··············

Celebrate

*"Listen. Listen to the Wind Words, the Spirit blowing
through the churches. I'm about to call each conqueror to
dinner. I'm spreading a banquet of Tree-of-Life fruit,
a supper plucked from God's orchard."*
REVELATION 2:7 MSG

Celebrate

*I came so that everyone would have life,
and have it in its fullest.*
JOHN 10:10 CEV

Did the angels throw a party when Jesus was born? Did they celebrate when He returned to Heaven after His death, resurrection, and ascension? I'm sure the heavens missed Him when He went to Earth.

The symbols of Christmas point to a future party we'll participate in, all because Jesus stepped off His celestial throne and clothed Himself with human flesh. The tree with its glittering ornaments represents eternal life; presents symbolize spiritual gifts of peace, joy, and love; the meal we share on Christmas Day foreshadows a breathtaking feast which all believers will enjoy.

Soon, our Savior and Bridegroom will return in power and might. He will destroy evil and bring justice on the earth. He will establish a Kingdom that will never end, where there will be no more war, racism, genocide, poverty, or despair.

Scripture doesn't give every detail about how or when Jesus' second coming will occur, but we know the answer to the most important question: *Who?* The eternal King will reign in glory, and every knee will bow to Him. We will finally, finally, be with our Bridegroom.

What began in Bethlehem will end in the New Jerusalem, and we will be there. We will sit at the table with Him, hardly able to contain our joy. It will be consummation of all our deepest hopes and dreams.

This picture stirs our hearts and quickens our spirit. We long for that day with groans that words can't express.

Come quickly, Lord Jesus. Amen.

Jesus, King of kings, Alpha and Omega, I long for Your return. I see the way we humans treat each other, and my soul pines for Your justice. My own body creaks and aches, and I am impatient for healing. Most of all, loving Bridegroom, I am filled with desire for Your presence. I will fall to my knees in admiration and praise. I can't wait for You to pick me up, hold me in Your arms, cup my face with Your hands, and wipe away the tears I will shed when I see You: the promise of Christmas, fulfilled.

You make known to me the path of life;
you fill me with joy in your presence,
with eternal pleasures at your right hand.
PSALM 16:11 NIV

10 Ways to Bless Others This Christmas:

1. Go to a Build-a-Bear Workshop[41] and create a stuffed toy to donate to a child in need.
2. Host a talent show and have audience members donate canned goods as their admission fee.
3. Hold a birthday party for Jesus—complete with balloons, cake, and prizes—and invite children from your neighborhood.
4. Get together with friends and make a blanket or quilt for someone who's been sick.
5. Have flowers delivered to the family of your church's youth, music, or children's pastor.
6. Pack a basket of holiday-themed goodies and deliver it to your favorite local physician.
7. Instead of giving each other gifts, go on a family mission trip over Christmas.
8. Send a fruit or cookie bouquet to a loved one with a Christmas birthday (they often get overlooked).
9. Cut your hair for Locks of Love.[42]
10. Raise money to fund clean water wells in Africa.[43]

NOTES

1. http://www.samaritanspurse.org/

2. http://www.salvationarmyusa.org/

3. Renner, Rick. *Sparkling Gems from the Greek: 365 Greek Word Studies for Every Day of the Year to Sharpen Your Understanding of God's Word* (Tulsa: Teach All Nations/Harrison House, 2003), 142.

4. Starbuck, Margot. *Surprised by a Loving God* (Grand Rapids: Baker Books, 2014), 162.

5. http://www.dressemberfoundation.org/

6. http://wish.org/

7. http://www.rmhc.org/season-of-giving

8. Morgan, Robert J. *Come Let Us Adore Him: Stories Behind the Most Cherished Christmas Hymns* (Nashville: J. Countryman, 2005), 68.

9. http://www.cefonline.com/

10. http://www.ymcafw.org/hood-county/default.aspx

11. http://www.habitat.org/

12. http://www.celebraterecovery.com/

13. http://www.worldvision.org/

14. Numbers 1, 2, and 3 are from http://qideas.org/articles/why-advent-is-not-business-as-usual/

15. http://www.shoesfororphansouls.com/about-mission.shtml

16. http://www.operationwarm.org/

17. http://hopeforjustice.org/abolition-groups/

18. http://www.presidentialprayerteam.com/index.php

19. Luke 1:29, 2:19, 2:33, 2:48

20. https://www.facebook.com/pages/Nancy-Franson-Writer

21. http://shoesfororphansouls.org/

22. http://www.wmu.com/index.php?q=ministries/cmjc/cwjccmjc-job-readiness

23. http://www.toysfortots.org/default.aspx

24. https://www.eridashare.com/

25. http://en.wikipedia.org/wiki/List_of_tool-lending_libraries

26. http://littlefreelibrary.org

27. http://www.solehope.org/

28. https://www.vibellajewelry.com/

29. Renner, *Sparkling Gems from the Greek*, 772.

30. www.gideons.org

31. http://www.cellphonesforsoldiers.com/

32. http://www.prisonfellowship.org/programs/angel-tree/

33. http://www.umcs.org/chrismons/

34. http://www.kristinschell.com/the-turquoise-table/

35. http://www.wrnmmc.capmed.mil/PatientVisitors/SitePages/Career/Volunteer.aspx#holidaymail

36. http://www.bbbs.org/site/c.9iILI3NGKhK6F/b.5962335/k.BE16/Home.htm

37. Contact Catholic Charities (http://catholiccharitiesusa.org/) or World Relief (http://worldrelieffortworth.org/) in the nearest city.

38. http://www.mowaa.org/

39. This tip—along with many other creative ideas—appears in *77 Creative Ways Kids Can Serve* by Sondra Clark (Indianapolis: Wesleyan Publishing House, 2008).

40. This tip—and many other thoughtful ideas—comes from *A Field Guide for Everyday Mission: 30 Days and 101 Ways to Demonstrate the Gospel* by Ben Connelly and Bob Roberts Jr. (Chicago: Moody Publishers, 2014).

41. http://www.buildabear.com

42. http://www.locksoflove.org

43. http://www.bloodwater.org/

About the Author

A few of Dena Dyer's favorite things: Christmas music, talking and laughing with her sons, date nights with her hubby, reading, cooking, and watching movies. In between helping her two boys with homework and shuttling them to church and school, she writes, speaks, and teaches English at her youngest son's homeschool co-op.

Dena's publishing credits include the books *Wounded Women of the Bible: Finding Hope When Life Hurts*, *Let the Crows' Feet and Laugh Lines Come*, *Mothers of the Bible*, *The Groovy Chicks' Road Trip* series, and *Grace for the Race: Meditations for Busy Moms*. Her articles have appeared in *Writer's Digest*, *Woman's World*, *Home Life*, and many other magazines, and her tips have been published in *Working Mother*, *Thriving Family*, *Redbook*, *Family Circle*, *Parenting*, *Nick Jr.*, and *Scholastic Parent*. For more information, visit her website/blog (www.denadyer.com) or connect with her on Facebook (denadyerauthor) or Twitter (motherinferior2).